MANAGING OLDER WORKERS

Overcoming Myths and Stereotypes

Gordon F. Shea

A FIFTY-MINUTE™ SERIES BOOK

CRISP PUBLICATIONS, INC.
Menlo Park, California

MANAGING OLDER WORKERS
Overcoming Myths and Stereotypes

Gordon F. Shea

CREDITS:
Editor: **Kay Kepler**
Typesetting: **ExecuStaff**
Cover Design: **Carol Harris**
Artwork: **Ralph Mapson**

Copyright © 1994 Crisp Publications, Inc.
Printed in the United States of America.

English language Crisp books are distributed worldwide. Our major international distributors include:

CANADA: Reid Publishing, Ltd., Box 69559—109 Thomas St., Oakville, Ontario Canada L6J 7R4. TEL: (416) 842-4428, FAX: (416) 842-9327

AUSTRALIA: Career Builders, P.O. Box 1051, Springwood, Brisbane, Queensland, Australia 4127. TEL: 841-1061, FAX: 841-1580

NEW ZEALAND: Career Builders, P.O. Box 571, Manurewa, Auckland, New Zealand. TEL: 266-5276, FAX: 266-4152

JAPAN: Phoenix Associates Co., Mizuho Bldg. 2-12-2, Kami Osaki, Shinagawa-Ku, Tokyo 141, Japan. TEL: 3-443-7231, FAX: 3-443-7640

Selected Crisp titles are also available in other languages. Contact International Rights Manager Tim Polk at (800) 442-7477 for more information.

Library of Congress Catalog Card Number 92-54364
Shea, Gordon F.
Managing Older Workers
ISBN 1-56052-182-1

This book is printed on recyclable paper with soy ink.

ABOUT THIS BOOK

Managing Older Workers is not like most books. It stands out in an important way. It is not a book to read—it is a book to *use*. The "self-paced" format and many worksheets encourage readers to get involved and try new ideas immediately.

This book introduces managers to the concept of an age-neutral workplace where hiring, training and promotion opportunities are not influenced by age. Use of the comprehensive strategies and tactics presented can dramatically improve your ability to draw out the best in your older workers.

Managing Older Workers (and other titles listed in the back of this book) can be used effectively a number of ways. Here are some possibilities:

- **Individual Study.** Because the book is self-instructional, all that is needed is a quiet place, committed time, and a pencil. By completing the activities and exercises, a reader receives both valuable feedback and action steps to improving managerial skills.

- **Workshops and Seminars.** This book was developed from hundreds of interactive seminars and contains many exercises that work well with group participation. The book is also a refresher for future reference by workshop attendees.

- **Remote Location Training.** This book is an excellent self-study resource for managers, supervisors, and managerial candidates not able to attend "home office" training sessions.

Even after this book has been used for training and applied in real situations, it will remain a valuable source of ideas for reflection.

Dedication—

To Brad, Mary and Trevor Shea

ABOUT THE AUTHOR

Gordon Shea is the president of PRIME Systems Company, a training and human resource development firm headquartered in Beltsville, Maryland. He has authored twelve books and over 200 research articles on management and employee development. These works range from how to negotiate win-win agreements that work, to building trust in the workplace and from a self-help book on time management to the Crisp workbook on Mentoring.

Mr. Shea is an accomplished trainer and public speaker who regularly presents seminars, workshops, and speeches on the subjects of his books.

Related to the topic presented in this book, he wrote *Managing Older Employees*, published by Jossey-Bass Publications Inc., in 1991.

Mr. Shea can be reached at:

> PRIME Systems Company
> P.O. Box 404
> Beltsville, MD 20705
> Phone: (301) 937-7230
> Fax: (301) 937-8588

Gordon F. Shea

Gordon F. Shea

CONTENTS

INTRODUCTION

Twelve Reasons to Take Older Employees Seriously

Managing our older workforce effectively is serious business for all of us, now and in our future. Here are the facts.

1. Older people are the fastest-growing segment of our workforce. Organizations will be increasingly dependent on the quantity and quality of these individuals to get the job done.

2. More than half of all retirees seriously need or would like to have some type of paid employment.

3. The baby boom generation has entered our older worker population, and will continue to swell each older segment of the workforce as the ''bulge'' moves forward.

4. Persons 40 years of age and older are a legally protected class of workers under the Age Discrimination in Employment Act (ADEA). This Equal Employment Opportunity law allows jury trials, liquidated damages and, in some cases, criminal penalties against individuals and organizations that discriminate against older employees.

5. More workers are filing age discrimination lawsuits—and some are winning big settlements.

6. Age bias and consequent age discrimination are so pervasive, ingrained and accepted in our society that they are very difficult to recognize, acknowledge and root out.

7. Many supervisory and personnel actions, such as reserving training and education opportunities for younger employees, tend to make older personnel obsolescent and less able to contribute, which damages the organization and the people in it.

8. Early retirement, previously often forced—now often rewarded—deprives our nation of an estimated $60–$80 billion a year in productivity. The rate of this loss is rising.

9. The number of younger workers aged 17–26 years, once considered our entry-level workforce, will decline 17 percent by the end of the decade, creating an even heavier dependence on older employees.

10. Employers who offer incentives for early retirement during recessions and layoffs often find their most productive workers leaving and at the same time the organization is initiating current and long-term pension expenditures to people likely to live longer than we ever dreamed.

11. Retirement income is not wealth. It is a call on wealth. Goods and services produced are wealth. Encouraged early retirement tends to have more money chasing fewer goods and services—the classic prescription for inflation, which can destroy the foundation of one's retirement income.

12. Older people are often a part of well-organized and powerful political action and voting blocks. They are quite capable of changing many of the rules organizations use in managing older personnel. Laws affecting the status of older workers are intimately tied to Social Security, health care and many other societal issues.

Anyone concerned with our nation's future should be concerned about how we manage our older workforce. But the older workforce is not an abstraction: It is, or will be, you and me.

P A R T

1

FACTS AND BIASES:

Promoting Age-Neutral
Work Policies

WORK OR RETIREMENT?
A PERSONAL DECISION

Work is "the physical or mental effort or activity directed toward the production or accomplishment of something desired by ourselves or others," but it is also much more than that. As individuals, we imbue "work" with attitudes, values and meanings that are highly personal. Our work also has social, economic and even political implications.

Even when there is a broad consensus about the value of "productive work" that "our workforce" does for pay, we all question the tasks, assignments and types of work, and the rewards, incentives and even propriety of some of the activities we perform.

Some of us lay claim to collections of work tasks and responsibilities as defined by an employer, which we call a job. Others define themselves by the type of work they do (I'm an electrician, I'm an engineer) and maintain that self-identity based on its associated skills and knowledge whether they are regularly employed, self-employed or unemployed.

Some individuals see their work as drudgery. They perform in an environment so oppressive that they virtually live to escape it. At the other end of the spectrum, some see what they do as a calling, a challenge and a self-enhancing form of discovery, which they tackle with enthusiasm and joy.

How we experience work, how we feel about it and even what others say about it influence whether we wish to continue it, offer it free as a volunteer or escape it altogether.

Retirement is a complex decision, and the choices related to it become more complex as our society and the options it offers become more varied. It was once considered adequate to classify adults as employed, unemployed or retired. This is a far too simple system of classification to use any longer.

Today we recognize that employed people may be "underemployed," involved in steady job-sharing arrangements or doing temporary daily, seasonal or project work, as well as holding "a regular job." "Unemployed people" may be changing their trade, location or occupation or taking part in a job training or educational program, and they may or may not be drawing unemployment compensation (government benefits based on a worker's previous employment). Finally, a "retired" person may be idle, working full-time, caring for family members, doing volunteer work, running for political office or engaged in virtually any other kind of activity imaginable.

HOW OLD IS OLD?

Some societies help their older members who no longer can work or provide for themselves. Other societies leave this responsibility to families or the charity of others. But when is a person too old to work? Or when is a person old enough to be eligible for Social Security benefits? Pension plans, laws and even informal agreements fix various age limits, but these are almost always arbitrarily set, unless disability is a factor. Key ages include:

38—(Approximately) for retirees from military service and some police, fire and similar organizations with 20-years-of-service retirement plans

40—When the Age Discrimination in Employment Act takes effect

55—When many private pension plans or company policies permit early retirement

62—For some forms of early retirement under Social Security, such as disability

65—Usual retirement age under the Social Security system

65–70—Bonus of 3 percent per year added to Social Security benefits if retirement is not taken at 65

70—Point at which Social Security payments are not affected by current earned income

Until recently, a federal age cap enabled some workers covered by federal law to work until age 70. Current Age Discrimination in Employment legislation has eliminated the age cap so that a covered person can continue working as long as his or her performance meets requirements.

AGE DISCRIMINATION

Studies show that managers are likely to engage in age discrimination without knowing it. One study surveyed 1,570 subscribers of the *Harvard Business Review* (virtually all of whom were in management) to assess how age considerations affect managerial decisions. Respondents were divided into two groups and each group was asked to evaluate problems involving poor worker performance and decisions regarding training and promotion. The problems presented to the two groups were identical except for the age of the employee involved in the incident—one-half involved a younger worker and the other half an older one.

In each situation, the older person fared worse in the evaluation regardless of her or his qualifications. When both the older and younger worker failed to perform the job, the older worker was seen as resistant to change and the respondents recommended reassignment. The survey respondents assessing the younger worker believed that he/she could benefit from an ''encouraging'' talk. But the older (equally qualified) worker was perceived as less motivated to keep up with changing technology, less creative and less able to cope with job-related stress. Age was the only variable in the study, yet this variable led to different treatment for the same offenses.

A later, similar study of 142 managers found that these managers were more willing to suggest retirement to employees the closer they were to age 65, regardless of the individual's performance or sex.

Bias against age and older workers is particularly offensive because it:

- Operates at a very low (usually subconscious) level, often without holders being aware of their biases

- Appears to be based on presumed knowledge, which is reinforced daily by comments of the people around us, that we become less able as we age

- Doesn't single out a group that is inherently different from us: We all expect to get older and, although it may sadden us, time does march on

AGE DISCRIMINATION (continued)

The assumption that we lose our abilities as we get older is inherently false, but leads many people to conclude that any kind of decline, whether or not the decline is job related, is a sign that they are "over the hill." These assumptions lead to what people consider to be common sense, and we get a multiplier effect of the self-fulfilling prophecy about age and aging individuals.

The road from age bias to discrimination is a short one. This road may also be a steep one, since few challenge the assumptions on which the biases are based. Therefore, it "makes sense" to encourage early retirement, plan for the future of only younger workers and lay off older workers in times of economic adversity without challenging the assumptions on which these decisions are made.

In reality, older employees usually get more capable as they get older; are our last great reserve of trained and dedicated workers and can often be creative, flexible and productive well into their eighties or nineties. Every day, major American companies such as Grumman, Travelers Insurance and Days Inn prove that older employees are good employees. Other organizations miss opportunities daily because of bias, ignorance and discrimination against older workers.

FRAMING THE LEGAL ISSUES

Employers have been constrained in some of their policies, procedures and individual behaviors by the Age Discrimination in Employment Act (ADEA) of 1967. While age fairness in an organization should not be driven by the fear of discrimination suits, all personnel should be aware of the force of this law.

The ADEA has been amended twice. In 1978 jury trials in age discrimination lawsuits were provided, and in 1985 the age cap of 70 was removed, thereby effectively ending age-based mandatory retirement for workers covered by federal laws. When complemented by state and local laws, older workers are protected by a substantial set of legal rules within which supervisors, managers, human resource personnel, and policy makers at all levels must operate.

Congress stated the purposes of the ADEA as:

1. To promote employment of older persons based on their ability rather than age

2. To prohibit arbitrary age discrimination

3. To help employers and workers find ways of meeting problems arising from the impact of age on employment

   The ADEA intends to achieve age-neutral personnel decisions so that hiring, training, education, promotion, discipline and termination are not influenced by age unless there is a ''Bona Fide Occupational Qualification,'' (BFOQ) such as public safety, that overrides the age-neutral intent of the law. The law protects any employee 40 years of age and above.

AGE DISCRIMINATION AWARENESS EXERCISE AHEAD

ORGANIZATIONAL EFFORTS TO AVOID AGE DISCRIMINATION

Below are ways your organization can avoid or reduce the number of age discrimination complaints and lawsuits. Indicate whether or not you believe that your organization is pursuing such methods or "uncertain" if you don't know.

The Organization	Yes	No	Uncertain
Trains supervisors and managers to be age-fair. Establishes realistic job criteria for each position.	☐	☐	☐
Has a performance-oriented, clear and specific performance appraisal system.	☐	☐	☐
Uses performance testing rather than paper and pencil tests for hiring.	☐	☐	☐
Uses age-neutral policies and procedures.	☐	☐	☐
Focuses attention on positive contributions that are made by older employees.	☐	☐	☐
Takes advantage of special attributes of older employees, including experience, mentoring, etc.	☐	☐	☐
Is age-neutral in all personnel actions.	☐	☐	☐
Documents a track record of efforts to prevent age discrimination.	☐	☐	☐
Organization uses a "progressive" disciplinary system.	☐	☐	☐
Uses an internal grievance or arbitration system to resolve disputes.	☐	☐	☐
Avoids citing age preferences (direct or indirect) in advertisements.	☐	☐	☐
Determines that older employees constitute a fair proportion of the workforce in all units where appropriate.	☐	☐	☐

The Organization	Yes	No	Uncertain
Posts ADEA law notices in conspicuous locations.	☐	☐	☐
Has no age information required on application forms. If age is specified in job requirements, a bona fide occupational qualification exists.	☐	☐	☐
Ensures that age neutrality applies to the treatment of all employees, including supervisors and managers.	☐	☐	☐
If discharge is unavoidable, considers voluntary retirement or resignation as an option.	☐	☐	☐
When discharge is considered, ensures that the replacement person is measurably superior in work performance.	☐	☐	☐
Employs older employees in personnel positions where decisions are made.	☐	☐	☐

Review your answers to determine if ''nos'' were checked more often than ''yeses.'' For each no checked, write down at least one possible action you and/or your company can take to correct the problem. For each ''uncertain'' checked, contact your human resource director and get the answer.

_____

_____

_____

_____

_____

_____

P A R T

2

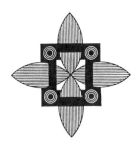

ASSESSING PRODUCTIVITY AND PERFORMANCE:

Managing for Success

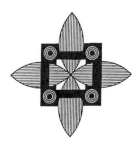

PRODUCTIVITY AND AGE

The time is past when we can simply measure productivity by the number of units a machine tool produces, the inches of weld a robot lays down, or the number of entries a data clerk makes in an hour. These days, the quality of the work is just as important. An experienced auto mechanic of 70 may return to his employer several times the value in marketable labor than an 18-year-old apprentice might, even taking wage differentials into account. An older salesperson may be able to outsell a younger competitor because of depth of product knowledge, empathy and persistence of effort.

Studies show that the greater an individual's experience, skills, competence and involvement in the work, the less a person's productivity will decline with age. For example, a study of 667 garment workers in the mid-1980s examined productivity, absenteeism, accidents and turnover. The workers were divided into six age categories; 212 employees held jobs requiring speed and 455 held jobs requiring skill. The researchers hypothesized that declines in physical ability with age would be greater on speed jobs than skill jobs. However, older workers surpassed the younger workers on both speed and skill jobs. Older workers in this study also had a lower rate of absenteeism, accidents and turnover than younger employees.

Older workers additionally may have characteristics that especially help an organization. A fairly consistent aspect from the literature on older workers is that they are generally credited with being good at teaching, coaching, counseling, craftwork and filling administrative positions. Working with younger people in a mentoring role is also often a value attributed to them. Three other attributes are often attributed to older people.

> **MATURITY**
> **SYNTHESIS**
> **CREATIVITY**

PRODUCTIVITY AND AGE (continued)

Identify the types of training, education or development activities that could be used to enhance a person's abilities in these three areas.

| Maturity | —the ability to make sound judgments.

Developmental Suggestions: _____

_____

_____

_____

_____

_____

| Synthesis | —the ability to build new, comprehensive systems of thought based on a lifetime's collection of observations, facts and viewpoints.

Developmental Suggestions: _____

_____

_____

_____

_____

| Creativity | —the ability to improvise and develop new ideas based on experience.

Developmental Suggestions: _____

_____

_____

_____

_____

KEEPING OLDER EMPLOYEES PRODUCTIVE

All too often, employers give up on older workers before they're ready to give up working. Older workers may need different things from the organization than younger people. Work-oriented preretirement training as part of the organization's career counseling could help determine each person's needs or wants before and after retirement. This could also increase employees' awareness of options, the need for planning and the realization that the need to be productive does not stop at a specific age.

From what you know of preretirement training programs, assess (if you can) the percentage of time spent on the option of continuing to work for the same organization:

_____

_____

_____

_____

_____

_____

_____

_____

An important part of keeping employees productive is to encourage them to contribute their ideas, experience, insights and opinions. This works best when people listen to them, treat their input with respect, encourage their contributions and strive to use their ideas.

These contributions serve a two-fold purpose:

#1. They are the lifeblood of any organization that competes for its prosperity and survival—and this includes government agencies competing for tax and budget funds. This competition appears to be intensifying, and the need for an enhanced flow of ideas and information is becoming more critical.

#2. These contributions, plus increased responsibility, recognition, the opportunity to achieve, and the work itself, can be positive motivators for virtually any employee, but are especially important to get and keep the older worker highly productive.

KEEPING OLDER EMPLOYEES PRODUCTIVE (continued)

Organizations can keep older employees productive in much the same ways other employees are kept productive. These include creating a positive environment in which employees:

Feel They Are ''In On Things''

Experience Positive Challenges

Are Recognized for Their Contribution

Participate in the Work Team

Are Offered Opportunities for Advancement

Employees also want to be free of the distractions and limitations of some workplaces, such as:

Job Insecurity

Oppressive Policies and Procedures

Unresolved Conflict with Supervisors and Coworkers

Negative Stress

Meaningless, Dead-end Work

List some things the employer might do to make the work environment more congenial for older workers.

_____

_____

_____

_____

_____

Exercise: Ensuring Success

1. Worker productivity in our knowledge society is more difficult to measure than it was when one could count the number of widgets produced in an hour. *Indicate three ways we might assess individual productivity in a knowledge environment.*

A. _____

_____

_____

B. _____

_____

_____

C. _____

_____

_____

2. Excellent supervisors today are sensitive to the needs, talents, experience and ideas of those who work for them. *Identify three ways in which supervisors can ensure the greatest contribution by older workers.*

A. _____

_____

_____

B. _____

_____

_____

C. _____

_____

_____

EXERCISE (continued)

3. The following three areas of management responsibility particularly affect the continued output of older employees. *List ways these factors can be managed for best results with older employees.*

    A. *Workplace safety.*

_____

_____

_____

    B. *Personality or behavioral differences.* A supervisor may attribute an older employee's behavior, such as resisting change, slowness, indecisiveness, talkativeness or insensitivity, to age, when most of those habits have been with the person for decades.

_____

_____

_____

    C. *The younger supervisor problem.* For some younger supervisors, approaching older workers, communicating performance deficiencies or appraising their work can be very difficult.

_____

_____

_____

MANAGING TO PERFORMANCE STANDARDS

Since not every older employee produces adequately, the issue of fairly appraising individual performance, identifying the cause of inadequate performance and resolving these issues in an age-neutral context becomes critical. A constructive process for resolving issues of inadequate performance is to:

1. Establish the gap between output and the job requirements

2. Determine the cause

3. Decide whether the problem is temporary or long term

4. Inform the individual of the gap

5. Work cooperatively and creatively to resolve the problem

If this cooperative approach fails to enable the person to achieve standards, disciplinary action or termination may be necessary. However, that outcome should be the last option rather than the first and should be approached carefully. Ideally, the supervisor should persistently help the employee close any gaps between job performance and job requirements. The ability to generate an imaginative win-win outcome requires:

- mutual listening
- effective problem identification
- generating options
- selecting and testing answers

This type of problem solving tends to satisfy all needs and is a measure of managerial and employee job competence.

PERFORMANCE ENHANCEMENT REVIEW

The following questions can be answered from your personal or professional viewpoint. Use them to stimulate discussion. In each case, ask "How can I/we achieve the following goals for older personnel (past 40 years of age)?"

Conserve individual knowledge, skills and abilities: _____

_____

Avoid employee obsolescence: _____

_____

Ensure top individual performance: _____

_____

Evaluate performance fairly: _____

_____

Use another person's experience fully: _____

_____

Ensure that supervisors, managers and the organization meet the legal obligations placed on them by the Age Discrimination in Employment Act (ADEA):

_____

_____

Encourage them to stay up-to-date and continue their training and education:

_____

_____

Enhance their sense of self-worth and resolve issues of low motivation or morale:

_____

_____

Reexamine these questions and your answers when you have finished this workbook.

THE PERFORMANCE APPRAISAL SYSTEM

The performance appraisal system and its use should be the beginning of action, not the conclusion. Unfortunately, many supervisors consider the job done when they have appraised an employee's performance. After that, they let the wheels grind. Below are some general guidelines for taking fair and legal action. Assess your own situation regarding these guides.

Guidelines	Yes	No
1. Performance standards are clearly established and well known to all parties	☐	☐
2. Performance standards are fair, reasonable and related to necessary work	☐	☐
3. There are no factors such as faulty equipment or unsafe working conditions that affect performance	☐	☐
4. Work standards do not contain arbitrary, capricious or unnecessary components that favor one group over another	☐	☐
5. Any gap between job requirements and employee performance is documented and communicated to the employee	☐	☐
6. All employees doing similar work are evaluated according to the same standard	☐	☐
7. Management has made reasonable efforts to help the employee correct the performance problem	☐	☐
8. All aspects of an employee's performance have been documented, including the positive factors	☐	☐
9. All factors related to performance or output, including absences, tardiness and defects are documented	☐	☐
10. Documentation does not begin when the employee files a grievance, but starts when the performance becomes unsatisfactory	☐	☐

APPLYING THE APPRAISAL SYSTEM

The courts have generally not required that an organization have a formal employee performance appraisal system. However, the more thorough, fair and clear the basis for an adverse action can be established, the more likely the employer will be successful in fending off possible charges of age discrimination.

Generally, the courts seek three characteristics in appraisals:

REASONABLENESS
RELIABILITY
RELEVANCY

First, the system should have a clearly stated purpose and a goal of fairness and objectivity. Secondly, the system can be considered reliable if appraisals of the same individuals are ''consistent among different raters and over a period of time.'' They should contain few or no subjective factors, since these tend to distort the rating. But most importantly, the system should use only those aspects of the work that are necessary for effective job performance.

When a formal system is poor or unconvincing, supervisory testimony is often pitted against worker testimony. Often this then becomes an issue of the credibility of the supervisor. Consequently, supervisors often need extensive training in using the system and especially in writing narrative comments documenting performance deficiencies.

Learning to do professional performance appraisals is excellent preparation for advancement and increased responsibility.

AGE-FAIR EMPLOYMENT

Supervisory, management and human resource personnel should not be left
to guess at appropriate behavior when working with older employees.
Appropriate training in ADEA concerns can create a general sense of
organizational justice in the work environment. To lay a foundation for
resolving performance problems and building high performance output for
older employees, the following actions can remove obstacles, leaving room for
positive incentives and motivators to take effect.

Exercise: Problem Resolution

Actions	Done	To Do
Revise policies and procedures to ensure that they are age-neutral in tone and intent	☐	☐
Train supervisors and managers in the rights and protections of ADEA and how to handle personnel	☐	☐
Help supervisors, managers and other personnel to free themselves of any personal anti-age biases and assumptions	☐	☐
Develop uniform standards of performance and behavior for all employees who are subject to the appraisal system	☐	☐
Establish objective performance measures, communicate them to all affected personnel and help them achieve the required performance	☐	☐
Publicize the productive contributions older employees make to society and the organization	☐	☐

EXERCISE (continued)

Actions	Done	To Do
Balance the ''age-attribute scale'' by taking advantage of the special attributes of older employees' experience, insight, loyalty, etc.	☐	☐
Train older employees for new jobs, equipment and environments (teams, etc.)	☐	☐
Ensure that reasonable accommodation allows for a safe and productive environment for all employees	☐	☐
Strive to reconcile age-related differences between older and younger workers	☐	☐

RESIDUAL PRODUCTIVITY PROBLEMS

Many doctors believe that if people are sound at birth and their physical and emotional needs are met, health rather than illness should be their natural condition in life. Illness has a cause that needs to be found. Similarly, if a worker's output declines, it is the job of supervisors and managers to detect the motivational or other causes and assist the employee to overcome them. A decline in an older person's work should be taken as an oddity, not the norm.

For example, when 64 people were identified by their supervisors as doing just enough to get by (and protected by seniority, labor contracts or special status), it was found that all workers expressed anger about some offense in their past. While other factors were also included in their long-term efforts to get even with the company (such as grief over ''being cheated out of their future''), anger was the paramount source of their unwillingness to perform as well as they could.

When workers do not produce adequately, their supervisors should work diligently to discover the source of the problem and resolve it. Avoiding or tolerating a productivity problem seldom helps the employee or the organization.

What can supervisors do? Here are some possibilities for working with an employee.

Confront the Issue

Use a neutral description of the behavior that is bothering you. Tell the person the effect on you and how you feel about the situation.

Listen Carefully

Encourage the individual to talk and work through their feelings.

Help Employees Solve Their Problem

Do not take over the problem, rather support as much as you can any solutions the person proposes.

RESIDUAL PRODUCTIVITY PROBLEMS
(continued)

Three things to remember when helping:

1. Arguing or trying to persuade the person to accept your answer often generates resistance

2. Acknowledge the positive aspects of the performance (achieve balance in defining the problem)

3. Some people have given up on the idea of getting much out of their job. Apathy, despair and resentment are problems to be solved, not a sign of badness.

Select one person who didn't produce well or had a significant decline in output and describe how you might have worked with that person.

_____

_____

_____

_____

_____

_____

_____

_____

_____

_____

_____

CASE STUDY AHEAD

Case Study: Casey Jones

You manage a large statistical research department in a Fortune 500 firm. During recent layoffs, the company offered a generous ''early-out'' package for those over 55 who chose to retire. Management was shocked to find that many of their best employees snapped up the package, while many less able employees chose to hang on as long as possible.

You are particularly concerned about the decision to retire made by Casey Jones, a woman actuary who not only is a top performer but does such specialized work that it will be very difficult to replace her. When you mentioned your concern to Tim Buto in the Human Resources Department, he said, ''Do you know that our professional women are choosing to retire early at three times the rate of men in proportion to their number? Only 20 years ago we were under an affirmative action order because of a shortage of women and minorities in professional and managerial positions. We've made great strides since then, but these cutbacks could put us back to where we were then.''

The gender aspect of these older employee losses had not occurred to you until then. You scheduled a conference with Casey partly to see if she'd be willing to stay, but you also wanted to consult her on the ''women leaving'' issue since you value her judgment and often got useful suggestions from her. She said many professional women viewed their careers differently from men. ''Male managers and professionals often enjoy their work as challenging and rewarding and are consequently less interested in retiring. However, many professional women are underemployed considering their credentials, experience and abilities. They hold less demanding jobs, are paid relatively less for the work they do and frequently are in staff support jobs rather than in line positions— where the action is. Retirement for women in those circumstances can be a lot more appealing than it is for men.''

Case Study: Analysis and Development

If this happened in your organization, what actions might be taken to make the work, responsibilities, rewards and opportunities more responsive to the needs of older women? Try to avoid platitudes and focus on innovative actions management might take.

_____

_____

_____

_____

P   A   R   T

3

TRAINING AND DEVELOPMENT:

Enhancing Older Employees' Opportunities

PROVIDING LEARNING OPPORTUNITIES

Despite an increasing dependence on an older workforce, investing in the training, education and development of older employees is apparently one of the most difficult problems faced by supervisors and managers, because age discrimination lawsuits often involve the denial of training to older personnel. Such discrimination against employees in their late forties and beyond is not uncommon, and this reluctance to train increases rapidly the older the employee's age.

The rationale most commonly expressed is that investing time and money in training or updating employees who were approaching retirement was simply not good management. Management assumed that older employees were short-timers, whereas younger workers have decades of employment ahead of them in which such investment could be recouped.

Yet voluntary turnover is far greater among younger employees, and the organization's training investment in younger personnel makes such individuals more attractive to competitors. However, an employee of 55 might have 10, 20 or even 30 years to pay back the training investment, and voluntary turnover in those age brackets (except for retirement for those who choose it) is virtually nil.

Other prejudices are at work as well. Younger workers are considered inherently quicker, better able to grasp training content and more willing to apply new methods or techniques. It is also commonly believed that older workers are set in their ways, resistant to new learning, have poor memories and experience declining intellectual abilities as they age.

Since virtually all of these assumptions are discriminatory as well as demonstrably false, the challenge before us is to train, educate and update older employees so that their learning is effective and profitable.

EDUCATION + DEVELOPMENT – BIASES = SUCCESS

32

Exercise: Understanding the Problem

Indicate the best answer according to your own knowledge and belief.

	True	False	Partly True
1. We reach an intellectual peak in our twenties and then begin a slow decline in mental abilities.	☐	☐	☐
2. Older employees inherently resist training and development opportunities.	☐	☐	☐
3. "You can't teach an old dog new tricks" is an accurate assessment of reality.	☐	☐	☐
4. Older employees do not do well in classroom settings and drag down the performance of the rest of the class.	☐	☐	☐
5. The older a person is, the less interested he or she is in learning new things.	☐	☐	☐
6. Older personnel prefer lecture, rote learning and a very formal classroom structure.	☐	☐	☐
7. Learning abilities for many older personnel decline through lack of practice and stimulation.	☐	☐	☐
8. Older learners tend to resist testing, challenging learning styles and special attention.	☐	☐	☐
9. Older employees often have memory problems, are slow at grasping concepts and tend to ramble.	☐	☐	☐
10. Many older employees consider themselves beyond school age and fail to see the advantages of continuous learning.	☐	☐	☐

Items 1 through 5 are demonstrably false except in a few individual instances. Items 6 through 10 may be partly true in that some older individuals fall in these categories. However, even those individuals can overcome these problems with effective training programs and support.

OBSTACLES TO DEVELOPING KNOWLEDGE AND SKILLS

Most older people continuously adapt to changing realities as long as they live, and to do so requires new learning as they go along. Older people may be uninterested in learning some things and resistant to learning others—as most of us are. Yet considerable research indicates that most older employees are willing to learn "new tricks" or even invent them if they perceive gain from doing so and if the gains exceed what they are willing to invest.

Still, some factors make older learners different from younger ones. As generalizations, these factors include:

- A tendency to regard any type of testing as threatening

- A reluctance (among older men especially) to be involved in activities that are embarrassing or threaten their self-image

- An apprehensiveness over repeating the rote learning and evaluation procedures that many older employees associate with schooling

- Many of the newer educational methods such as team learning, games and small group training exercises may seem strange or even threatening to some older employees

- A low tolerance for training exercises and activities that seem remote from the purpose at hand

- Stress and insecurity when challenging or confrontational (rather than supportive) training techniques are used

- Performance is depressed most when the material is difficult or complex (this anxiety disappears once the material has been learned and is being reviewed)

- Being out of practice in learning situations may lead to low initial performance until the person gets back into the swing of things

- Past experience, beliefs and values that seem contrary to the new learning may have to be resolved before new learning is feasible.

Overall, we should recognize that most of these characteristics can be overcome by good training program design. For example, quality measures of attainment can be obtained by other methods than testing, and slower methods of learning don't mean poor results.

LEARNING STYLES AND PRODUCTIVITY

Some generalizations about how older employees learn can guide managers in designing effective training and educational programs. These include:

1. *An adjustment period may be necessary.*

Older workers who have been out of school for some time may need practice and training to rebuild learning skills. Refresher courses in study techniques, memory skills and writing can particularly help.

2. *Self-paced learning seems to work best with older employees.*

Self-paced learning methods, such as programmed instruction, are minimally stressful and noncompetitive. Students can master the correct responses at their own pace and then move on to new material. Doing so comfortably can lead to high performance on the job when older workers use the material learned.

3. *Adjusting methods and pace when unlearning and relearning are required.*

All of us have developed habits and investments (including emotional ones) in certain ways of doing things, as well as in the beliefs and ideas we cherish. To change these can be painful and we need time and opportunity to adjust. Explaining or demonstrating the change and the reasons for it early in the program and involving older personnel in planning the change can facilitate new learning and practice.

4. *Training materials should be relevant and related to the job.*

Older employees tend to have a low tolerance for material that they consider abstract or ''nice to know.'' For example, paper and pencil testing is often resented unless such calculations or paper work are or will be part of their regular work assignments.

5. *Learning assignments requiring memorization often require more practice.*

A few practice sessions produce long-lasting, high-performance results by older employees on memory-related tasks—results that can match the performance of much younger employees. The use of work-related checklists, algorithms and ''decision trees'' also can be used effectively to help workers remember tasks involving long chains of activities.

6. *Testing and evaluation stresses older employees so much that learning may fall off rapidly.*

Older personnel are particularly affected by concerns about looking bad before peers and maintaining their dignity and self-image. One of the reasons for relatively low test scores by some older personnel is the fear of being wrong, and therefore they may fail to answer at all rather than risk being wrong. They also do not like to be compared to others and learn best when measured against their own previous standards.

7. *Participative teaching techniques that accent the learner's previous accomplishments and experience produce high performance.*

Like most of us, older learners respond best to praise, recognition, rewards and an environment that is psychologically supportive. However, the change from the passive learning older workers may have experienced in the past to participation in the learning process may take time.

Learning ability most often declines through a lack of use of one's mind. Adults who continue to be involved in educational activities learn more effectively than those who do not. Therefore, employers who deny older personnel learning opportunities produce a negative downward spiral, a self-fulfilling prophecy. By contrast, we need to create opportunities to keep the older person's learning ability alive through developmental assignments and training opportunities.

SUCCESSFUL TEACHING TECHNIQUES

From an employer's perspective, the purpose of training and education is to produce successful job performance—not testing. Unfortunately, many program designers do things that make learning difficult for older learners and overlook their need for demonstrable success. The following list contains guides to effective training for virtually any population. However, if an examination of the training design is made with older employees specifically in mind, their special needs are more likely to be considered.

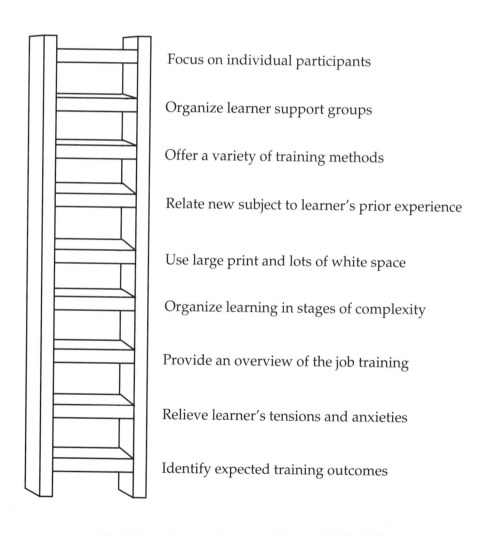

Focus on individual participants

Organize learner support groups

Offer a variety of training methods

Relate new subject to learner's prior experience

Use large print and lots of white space

Organize learning in stages of complexity

Provide an overview of the job training

Relieve learner's tensions and anxieties

Identify expected training outcomes

LADDER TO LEARNING SUCCESS

TRAINING PROGRAM DESIGN CONSIDERATIONS

Diversity in learning needs and styles tends to be far greater among older work groups and among older individuals than in the population in general. This diversity may both require and allow for greater flexibility in teaching approaches, more options in media and methods and more attention to individual backgrounds and needs. Focusing on such differences can enhance training payoffs in older learning populations.

▶ *Generational differences.* More formal schooling is needed today than at the beginning of the century to get a good job, and increased technological complexity and work specialization have caused increases in training level needs. With our older workforce spanning decades, generational differences in training, education and skill levels need to be taken into account.

▶ *Cognitive styles.* How we learn is often related to the type and extent of our highest educational level achieved and training experiences. In general, this means that the further we go in school not only do we learn new material but we master new ways to absorb that new material. Often a person will settle on a personal cognitive style and use that approach to learning new material—often with limited success. Such a style may be related to generational differences. Thus, poor reasoning ability may not be an inherent problem but rather a lack of knowing how to handle data efficiently or reason systematically.

▶ *Prior learning and experiences.* When we consider a potential older workforce spectrum of 40 or more years, the generational contrasts can be enormous. Each person's prior learning is a valuable resource and should be built upon and used whenever possible. It may be necessary to broaden some employees' background, perceptions and experiences before he or she can contribute their best to new learning experiences.

▶ *Gender, culture and ethnic differences among older employees.* Differences in learning patterns between older males and females in our own culture may result from the socialization process they were exposed to as children. Similarly, recent immigrants or workers whose first language is not English may expect (and even demand) greater focus on lectures, rote learning and even negative criticism.

Attention to factors of workforce diversity will yield greatest training results.

4

MOTIVATION AND MORALE:

Encouraging Maximum Performance

MOTIVATION AND MORALE

Personal productivity or the lack of it is a direct consequence of a person's motivation and morale. When an older employee does only enough to get by or seeks early retirement, supervisors may assume that it is the fault of the worker. They fail to see how their own behavior affects the equation. Of course, it does.

Employers should arrange policies and incentives to encourage high performance of their older employees and encourage their leaders to behave in ways that permit and encourage high productivity levels and motivation for all their employees. Older employees respond to some motivators very much as younger people do, but also react quite differently than their younger associates do to other policies, incentives and managerial behaviors. For example, money is often perceived as a motivator, but we only need to ask ''How much?'' and ''For what?'' to see that its power is not absolute, or that a given amount will affect different people differently. Time-and-a-half for overtime might affect one person powerfully, but scarcely influence another person at all.

Keys to Motivation and Morale

Three aspects of motivation and morale tend to be important for older workers.

1. *Virtually all motivation is self-motivation and very personal.*

You can't really motivate anyone but yourself. Management may offer punishment or rewards for certain types of behavior, but the individual chooses whether or not to respond to them and to what degree.

When we speak of motivating another person, we are engaging in omnipotent fantasies. Though the incentives or disincentives offered by management may elicit the desired response because employees may decide to go along, they do so for their own purposes. Furthermore, some people have been raised to respond to certain incentives and therefore they believe that they must comply.

Experienced employees have often learned to cut a finer line between the incentive and what they offer in return. Yet that very experience enables them to give much more than management dreams, if the employees choose to do so.

MOTIVATION AND MORALE (continued)

2. *Motivation also can be positive or negative.*

Many highly motivated employees take care of their own needs, withhold knowledge or ideas, or pursue personal agendas. Older employees who are resentful about past unfairnesses, feel their abilities discounted or believe that they are trapped may return much less to the organization than they are capable of giving.

3. *Motivation and morale are quite different.*

Motivation incites action because it tends to be goal-oriented. It is often specific and focused.

Morale is more general and often is the result of a variety of events or factors. When morale is low, a lassitude develops and energy lags. Morale also frequently has a social or group dynamic involved and does not necessarily drop during difficult times. A feeling of personal or group power may determine whether morale is high or low. A sense of ability to master adversity is the key.

Employer policies and practices can influence individuals or groups and, although they will choose which and when to respond to them, older employees may need a more complicated approach than we initially expect. Experienced workers have longer and more complex histories, and the incentives and effort required to get a positive individual response from an older person may need to be more subtle and intricate.

Motivation		Morale
Goal Oriented	>—<	General
Individual	>—<	Group
Direction	>—<	Mood

THE PARADOX OF MOTIVATION AND MORALE

List three supervisory behaviors or incentives that would allow an older employee to be motivated constructively.

a. _____

_____

b. _____

_____

c. _____

_____

List three supervisory behaviors or disincentives that would tend to alienate an older employee.

a. _____

_____

b. _____

_____

c. _____

_____

List three types of policies or practices that would tend to damage older worker morale.

a. _____

_____

b. _____

_____

c. _____

_____

THE PARADOX OF MOTIVATION AND MORALE (continued)

List three policies or practices that would tend to elevate older employee morale.

a. _____

_____

b. _____

_____

c. _____

_____

Identify three inconsistencies you have observed between what an organization claims to be its goals and its actions and practices.

a. _____

_____

b. _____

_____

c. _____

_____

OVERCOMING PAST DEMOTIVATORS

To design programs that offer incentives to older personnel to remain in the workforce and contribute their maximum to their employer, we need to understand older employees and what motivates them. Older employees may lose interest in their work when they receive a low performance rating unfairly, are left on a dull assignment too long or are passed over for promotions in favor of younger employees. Initially older workers may strive to improve their output, but if their efforts seem to produce no results, despair, indifference and lowered self-esteem quickly set in. Older employees treated this way tend to become pessimistic about their future and expect little reward for extra effort. On project work especially, where individual performance standards are unclear and personal output is hard to measure, judgment about an individual's contribution is often subjective. Older personnel may feel they have less job mobility and thus are trapped in a bad situation.

How can these discouraging tendencies be overcome? First, of course, is just to stop discriminatory practices. Managers, however, can help their employees stay motivated in other ways.

► **Asset Counseling**

This technique helps older employees inventory their personal and job-related assets and experiences, which can enhance self-image and job counseling efforts.

► **Preventing Obsolescence**

An organizational philosophy of lifelong learning can keep employees sharp and lessen the likelihood of a drop in performance because of obsolescence.

► **Time Off for Study**

Sabbaticals, residential programs, and other variations of fairly long-term, full-time study may be necessary to keep a high-tech workforce in shape; new skills that are difficult to master on a part-time or short-term basis can serve as both a reward and an incentive for older personnel.

OVERCOMING PAST DEMOTIVATORS
(continued)

► Achievement Motivation Training

Training that elicits and reinforces patterns of thinking and behaving that characterize high achievers produces noticeable behavioral improvement in 60%–70% of course participants within the following year; older employees (over 55) benefited as much as younger ones from such training.

► Performance Appraisal Systems that Focus on the Future

Ranking employees against each other produces losers, and a focus on past failure destroys the anticipation of success and rewards; by contrast, a focus on future positive achievements motivates workers to do better.

► Supervisory Support and Encouragement

The peer reinforcement that normally comes from including older employees in on-the-job training is one of the best ways to prevent obsolescence and cure motivational problems. Serious consultation with older personnel often reveals an interest in learning new types of work, practicing new skills and even entering a new career field—a positive response to any of which could overcome lassitude and indifference.

Providing objective information on work options, training and transfer opportunities can reawaken the spark of interest so often lacking in older employee work situations—assuming, of course, that older personnel have a truly fair opportunity to achieve success in new situations.

ACHIEVEMENT MOTIVATION TRAINING

Achievement motivation has been found to decline very sharply after age 40 because workers believe that job success is impossible or meaningless, their abilities will decline soon and incentives, rewards and challenges are reserved for the young. It is possible to survey levels of achievement motivation. Think of a typical older employee in your organization and assess his or her level of motivation based on these factors.

People who have a high level of achievement motivation	Your assessment
1. They see themselves as potent in their work	
2. Are quite active	
3. Are future oriented	
4. Want to take personal responsibility	
5. Are willing to take moderate (calculated) risks	
6. Want specific, concrete feedback on their results	
7. Take pride in their accomplishments	

Achievement Motivation Training

- Encourages self-confidence

- Stimulates and reinforces achievement thinking

- Provides an easy-to-use way of expressing inner thoughts and feelings

- Uses games and simulations to enhance self-understanding

- Encourages personal goal setting

- Provides group support

- Enables employees to confront negative behavior in the organizational climate

Achievement motivation training can enhance the organizational climate for all employees, yet results are especially effective in overcoming late career lassitude.

5

TEAMWORK AND LEADERSHIP:

Maximizing Older Workers' Contributions

DEVELOPING PRODUCTIVE WORK TEAMS

As the technological complexity of our workplaces increases, employers will need more genuine teamwork in more complex environments than ever before. This raises the questions of: "Does age make a difference in meeting our need for cooperative work group efforts, and if so, what can be done to maximize the contribution of older employees?"

Research indicates that there is a generational problem for some older personnel in performing some types of work in groups. Our tradition of individual contribution rather than team effort, deference to authority or status and interpersonal competition rather than cooperation may be more the norm for older generations. Younger workers are more familiar with cooperative task efforts in their training and educational experiences. Consequently, younger groups tend to be more effective in discovering and using the special knowledge and skills of their group members.

An important factor in this superior younger group performance was their flexibility in shifting leadership on each decision to a group member who could best handle that item. In older groups, researchers often found that many individual members were more interested in preserving status, exercising (or avoiding) leadership and not looking bad to their peers. These individuals tended not to share their knowledge nor contribute much to group discussion.

Although group trust and experience with group problem-solving processes are critical in determining group effectiveness, poor supervision and age discrimination were likely to have undermined older-group performance. A tendency by many older managers to dictate decisions is based on the learned expectation that decisions are best made solo.

By contrast, starting with their academic studies, younger people often have far more experience in group process work and group decision making than older workers do. They appear (generally) to be less concerned with status and control, less competitive in a group setting and more able to focus on achieving optimum results than some older individuals.

These realities reveal learned responses that can be overcome with training and greater experiences in group problem-solving activities. Since these differences are generational—that is, attributable to the way a person was raised, educated and socialized in the workplace—there is no inherent reason why these habits cannot be overcome. Where older persons are expected to operate in and contribute to group achievements, they may need to be trained and counseled in how to become better group contributors.

OBSTACLES TO EFFECTIVE TEAMWORK

Some older personnel may respond well to an offer of training or help in adapting to an increase in team activities—such as when moving to self-directed work teams or when total quality management initiatives are introduced—while others may not. Assessing a need for training or help may be facilitated by using the following statements to examine a person's comfort level with group activities.

Previous Experience	Seems to be a factor
I am not used to participating as a team member except in competitive situations	☐
I believe that informal groups or teams are generally cliques and should be avoided	☐
Work on my job has been organized for individual contribution, and cooperation has been discouraged	☐
Cooperation has been seen as conforming, not getting in the way and rarely giving help	☐
A team player is one who agrees with the supervisor does not argue and plays their assigned role	☐
Volunteering help is taboo, an insult or to be treated with suspicion	☐
Asking for help is a sign of weakness or dependency	☐
We relied on experts, which leads to passivity in the presence of such people	☐
Teamwork is seen as any meeting in which we agree that the problem was solved, regardless of the consequences	☐
Agreeing for the sake of avoiding conflict is considered to be acceptable behavior	☐
Even when intellectually committed to teamwork, we may lack the skill to make it work	☐
I feel vaguely uncomfortable or impatient with all the talk associated with group problem solving	☐

IDENTIFYING SOURCES OF CONFLICT

Leadership abilities are most challenged when managers face unfamiliar problems. In examining the relationship between older and younger employees, we encounter several potential conflicts, including:

► *Generational conflicts of values.* Supervisors will detect age-based hostility most often by listening for generalizations that are expressed as absolutes. Such generalizations are almost always false, and confronting them can be critical in building an effective workforce.

► *Resentment of seniority.* In organizations in which seniority counts, older workers are likely to gain relative advantage when an economic downturn or layoff looms. It is not uncommon to experience spontaneous bickering or other negative behaviors that unsettle employees at these times.

► *Economic Competition.* Layoffs, ''pressured'' early retirement, or early retirement incentives can lead to age-related competition, legal actions and even sabotage.

► *Blocking Advancement of Younger Employees.* As older employees stay longer in organizations, younger workers may believe that the ''old-timers'' are holding jobs they don't need.

► *Increased Competition.* Since ADEA legislation and the Americans with Disabilities Act were passed, the potential for competition from these and other protected classes has increased, and since a given individual may be covered by more than one type of protection, the situation will become increasingly complex as our workforce ages.

► *Privilege and Status.* When a group loses status or privileges or when others gain in a relative sense, the ''losers'' will often resent the ''winners,'' even if the loss is only perceptual. Often such groups need advanced explanations and a chance to talk through their feelings.

► *Illness and Handicap Conflict.* Strange as it may seem, sometimes supervisors and coworkers cause trouble for employees who survive a major illness such as cancer, stroke or heart attack and return to work. It seems to be taken as an embarrassment by some other people in the workforce.

Conflict-resolution techniques may be needed to handle such problems if they increase in the future.

Exercise: Age Conflict and Its Resolution

From your own experience, or from the seven sources of age conflict, identify three problems that might (or have) occurred in your work group. Then list the interventions one could make to lessen or resolve such conflicts.

1. **Type of age conflict** _____

_____

_____

_____

  Ways to lessen or resolve such conflict _____

_____

_____

_____

2. **Type of age conflict** _____

_____

_____

_____

  Ways to lessen or resolve such conflict _____

_____

_____

_____

3. **Type of age conflict** _____

_____

_____

_____

  Ways to lessen or resolve such conflict _____

_____

_____

_____

Case Study: A Team Approach

You have recently been put in charge of a technical team of people who have previously worked for years as individual contributors in their professional specialties. The team has been assigned a "crash" project that is vital to organizational success in a new market area. Each team member brings valuable specialized knowledge and experience to the team, and your job is to integrate their special abilities and contributions to develop a product strategy. However, team cooperation, mutual respect, sharing information and generating creative ideas are in very short supply in this group, which must focus and work together to be successful.

You are having problems with all of the team members, who tend to see interpersonal competition as the norm for organizational life. At the moment you are engaged in writing training and development prescriptions for each person in the hope of effecting interventions that will help them see the consequences of their beliefs, attitudes and behaviors on team performance. If you can achieve that, you believe you can work out with each person a plan for what he or she need in the way of training, mentoring or support, for making the needed personal changes.

Before you are cards for the three oldest (all past 50) members of the group. These three could become the team's greatest assets because of their knowledge of the product lines, their experience with getting things done in the organization and the special technical insights they've gained over the years. However, now they are contributing little of their expertise. These individuals are Raul, Joyce and Bandar.

Raul is very concerned with status, respect and authority. He believes decision making should come from the leader and is impatient with discussion and irritated by debate—"a lot of useless talk," he says.

Joyce is the source of several important patents and technical innovations in the company. She takes a long time to produce something, but the results are often stunning when revealed. Often rambling in meetings, seemingly searching for a point she wants to make, she appears to have trouble synthesizing information at times.

Bandar has a very solid practical background and likes to work with his hands. He is exceptionally sensitive to people's feelings and needs. He likes to work alone much of the time and tends to be quiet and possibly passive. His ideas are more likely to come out in a written paper or report than in the group.

Case Study: Analysis and Development

Although people may not change their personality significantly, they can often modify their behavior if the anticipated gains are great enough. Thus introverts can engage in extroverted behavior if they choose to and know how to do it. Substitution of one learned behavior for another can also be done if the incentives to do so are great enough. We change our general behavior patterns all the time, even if we go back to our original preferred state later.

In writing prescriptions for development for these three individuals, be as specific as you can about training or supportive activities that you can use to increase their adaptability in the team.

Raul

_____

_____

_____

_____

_____

Joyce

_____

_____

_____

_____

_____

Bandar

_____

_____

_____

_____

_____

LEADERSHIP OPPORTUNITIES FOR OLDER EMPLOYEES

Organizations are shifting from emphasizing management to focusing on leadership. Managing tends to stress organizing resources, being guided by policies and procedures and planning and controlling people and processes. Leading tends to pursue objectives, sometimes in a less constrained and more dynamic process for achieving organizational goals.

Leaders influence people to stretch themselves reasonably but progressively—to grow as the years roll on. When employees do so, they feel good about themselves, their jobs, their coworkers, their leaders and their organization.

Best Leaders

Over the years I have asked supervisors and managers to think of the best leader they have ever worked for and identify one thing that that person did or said that led to the individual being classed as a ''best leader.'' Below are the results. Identify those items that correlate to your ''best leader.''

Behaviors—Their best leader did or said	I can relate to this
1. Told me what was needed and let me do it my way	☐
2. Listened to my problems, personal or job-related	☐
3. Explained the job and asked for my ideas on how to do it	☐
4. Backed me up when I needed support	☐
5. Encouraged me to improve myself	☐
6. Gave me credit and praise when I did well	☐
7. Treated me with respect even when I erred	☐
8. Accepted me—it was comfortable going to him/her with a problem	☐
9. Set high but achievable standards and helped me meet them	☐

LEADERSHIP OPPORTUNITIES FOR OLDER EMPLOYEES (continued)

Behaviors—Their best leader did or said	I can relate to this
10. Was straight with me and kept his or her word	☐
11. Divided interesting and challenging work fairly	☐
12. Was personally well-organized (reduced uncertainty)	☐
13. Let me know about changes that affected me	☐
14. Constantly searched for easier, faster and less expensive methods	☐
15. Laid out the job carefully and explained it to us	☐

How do you perceive older workers would relate to these items?

The best leader:
Supports
Monitors
Acknowledges
Respects
Teaches

LEADERSHIP TECHNIQUES FOR MAXIMUM PERFORMANCE

High performance does not mean superhuman output or consistently remarkable achievements. However, it does mean that a person enthusiastically contributes whatever he or she can at a particular time to a particular situation and quite consistently does their best.

High performance also usually reflects a person's level of training, mastered skills, special experience and insights, imagination and ideas, personality and the power and energy the individual can generate and use in doing his or her jobs.

One measure of a leader is that person's ability to prepare, develop and inspire each employee to achieve high performance regardless of age. Effective leaders also focus on the future as well as their present because real leaders have to be leading people somewhere. Leaders today concern themselves with preventing obsolescence, identifying and responding to trends, anticipating problems, preparing their workforce to overcome obstacles, maximizing opportunities and envisioning, as well as they can, the working world of tomorrow.

Leadership, teamwork and the search for productivity generally converge at the first line of supervision—where management understands that in a complex world, leadership can come from several sources and most situations no longer require a single leader. In self-directed work teams, for instance, several persons may lead the team at different times and in different situations. In complex project management situations, special talents, experience or abilities may require that some individuals play a leading role in guiding groups to accomplish specific tasks or phases of the project. Older employees may be especially well-equipped to assume such leadership roles if they are properly prepared to do so.

P A R T

6

WORK POLICIES AND FLEXIBILITY:

Creating Alternative Work Programs

THE IMPORTANCE OF FLEXIBLE WORK POLICIES

The key to continued employment of many older workers at appropriate salary and skill levels largely depends on alternative work arrangements. Unfortunately, management is often wedded to employing people only for full-time jobs. Employers also assume that presence is essential to productivity and cannot assess the value of a person's contribution except in terms of hours expended. Consequently, many older workers view retirement as a one-way chute—down and out.

Flexible work policies can pay dividends to our society by allowing people to continue contributing to the national wealth and their own income, health and well-being without maintaining a full-time job when they are eligible for retirement. Organizations benefit by conserving expertise, using people who know the business and the organization and by avoiding the training and break-in costs of hiring replacement employees.

ADJUSTING JOBS TO KEEP OLDER PEOPLE EMPLOYED

Older people who are still employed may need alternative work options to meet personal and family demands. It is increasingly common to find older employees who are still raising children or grandchildren and involved in taking care of aged parents as well. Additionally, many older persons want post-retirement work or would consider putting off retirement altogether if they were allowed one or more of the following options.

Check those options which are offered by your organization.

☐ Job sharing

☐ Flexible scheduling (flextime)

☐ Part-time employment (less than 30 hours of work per week)

☐ Consulting assignments

☐ Seasonal work

☐ Sabbaticals (without loss of seniority or benefits)

☐ "Tapered off" employment running to retirement over a period of months or years

☐ Short-term projects

☐ Compressed work week: 20 to 40 hours in two to four-day increments

☐ Reduced hours (even with reduced pay)

☐ Job rotation or flexible shifts

☐ Doing work at home

☐ Doing work at (nearby) computer centers

☐ Contracted work

☐ Partial pension/partial work plan

Such alternative work options offer employers many opportunities for cost savings, more balanced work loads and retention of expertise. At-home or project assignments may allow a person's expertise to be used only when needed. Similarly, many of these work arrangements have been found to reduce the on-the-job idleness often found in full-time jobs. Furthermore, it may be easier to judge the value of the work performed.

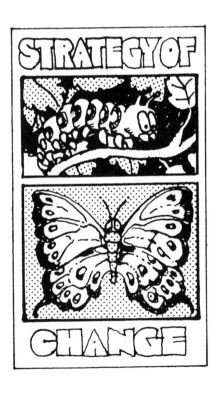

FLEXIBLE WORKPLACES

Creative work programs for older personnel seem limited only by our imagination. Some of these programs, however, go far beyond alternatives to conventional work arrangements. A sampling of existing programs illustrates the breadth and diversity of such special efforts.

Instron Instron, a maker of materials-testing equipment in Cambridge, Massachusetts, uses retired workers in its "sales emeritus programs" to coach younger salespeople. Sharing their experience in people skills and product knowledge reduces the "learning by mistakes" costs of younger salespeople. This approach is credited with producing quick and substantial results and shortening the training time.

Builders Emporium Builders Emporium has redesigned jobs to accommodate older workers and ensure their continued loyalty and presence. The job of store clerk was redesigned throughout the 121 California-based home centers to eliminate heavy lifting by assigning night crews to replenish shelves. Store clerks, who constituted about two-thirds of nearly 8,000 sales personnel, was recast to emphasize selling skills. Builders Emporium had found that older staff knew the merchandise better and had more experience working with customers. This change also reduced turnover rate and improved morale substantially.

Grumman Corporation Grumman has been a leader in using "job banks" and "retiree pools" that fill about 60 percent of the company's temporary employment needs. When an internal survey revealed that 50 percent of the company's retirees indicated that they would like to know about part-time and special project opportunities, the company established a temporary, part-time, on-call pool of Grumman retirees. Company officials have said "this is one of the dozens of ways we show that we value our older staffers."

Varian Associates Varian offers a retirement transition program that permits employees who are age 55 or older to work 20–32 hours a week as long as they and the company wish. This $1 billion-per-year high-tech equipment maker provides proportional benefits, partial medical and dental insurance, vacation and even, in some cases, stock options and profit sharing. Employees who had retired before the program was established could resume work under the plan as an alternative to full retirement or full employment.

| Polaroid Corporation | Polaroid has been classed as one of the most versatile employers of older workers. Flexible |

Polaroid has been classed as one of the most versatile employers of older workers. Flexible work alternatives have been credited with encouraging 30 percent of workers over 65 to stay on the job. Options include rehearsal retirement, tapering off, temporary or permanent part-time work, job sharing, flex-time, consulting contracts and a retiree pool for work during peak periods.

Corning Glass Works

Corning employs about 100 workers as senior associates. These individuals often serve as advisors, mentors, troubleshooters and back-up for managers and professionals in their specialized fields. Senior associates receive extra pay with these titles (8–12 percent is not uncommon), and few want to leave since it would mean a loss of such benefits.

Travelers Insurance Company

Travelers has an Office of Consumer Information that is completely staffed by 16 retired employees who job-share four positions and respond to 36,000 calls a year. Their other job banks have become so well-known that Travelers has opened them to retirees from other organizations who live in the area.

Kelly Services

Kelly has a special recruiting program called Encore for attracting and placing workers who are over age 55.

Manpower, Inc.

Manpower is the largest temporary agency in the world and claims that more than 25 percent of its 700,000 employees world-wide are older workers.

It is clear that many employers could do more to employ older personnel if they so desired. However, none of these programs is aimed at favoring older workers over younger ones. Employers simply want to ensure that human resources are not wasted and older employees simply want a level playing field in opportunity. Alternative work programs can provide that.

SUMMARY: WIN-WIN WORK OPTIONS

To many supervisors, managers and employees themselves, a job is a job, work is work and a task is a task without giving very much thought to who does it, how it is done and if it is being done in the best way—unless a problem arises. Unless competitive pressures force change, little real adjustment occurs in many organizations.

However, within a decade the primary competitive forces at work in the world will be between older workers in the technologically advanced societies in the world. Western Europe is already more dependent on older workers than we are. Japan is only a few years behind us. The industrialized nations of the Pacific Rim have societies in which older people are respected and valued, which may in time give them a competitive advantage as the experience of their workforce matures.

The more successful and competitive a society becomes in the global marketplace, the more rapidly its workforce ages. Third world nations tend to have young populations because disease, poor nutrition, inadequate health care and many other factors reduce life expectancies. Yet as these economies mature, so will the workforce.

One of our great challenges today is to establish flexible work options that conserve the most experienced portion of our workforce. The benefits of keeping such employees usually outweigh any costs, and the company is assured of qualified, experienced personnel especially when part-time, substitute or temporary workers are needed. Using our older workforce productively can make things work for the company, the employee and all of society.

NOTES

FOR OTHER FIFTY-MINUTE SELF-STUDY BOOKS
SEE THE BACK OF THIS BOOK.

NOTES

FOR OTHER FIFTY-MINUTE SELF-STUDY BOOKS
SEE THE BACK OF THIS BOOK.

NOTES

FOR OTHER FIFTY-MINUTE SELF-STUDY BOOKS
SEE THE BACK OF THIS BOOK.

NOTES

FOR OTHER FIFTY-MINUTE SELF-STUDY BOOKS
SEE THE BACK OF THIS BOOK.

NOTES

FOR OTHER FIFTY-MINUTE SELF-STUDY BOOKS
SEE THE BACK OF THIS BOOK.

$$\boxed{\textbf{NOTES}}$$

We hope you enjoyed this book. If so, we have good news for you. This title is part of the best-selling *FIFTY-MINUTE*™ *Series* of books. All *Series* books are similar in size and identical in price. Several are supported with training videos (identified by the symbol ⓥ next to the title).

FIFTY-MINUTE Books and Videos are available from your distributor. A free catalog is available upon request from Crisp Publications, Inc., 1200 Hamilton Court, Menlo Park, California 94025.

FIFTY-MINUTE Series Books & Videos organized by general subject area.

Management Training:

Management Training (continued):

Personal Improvement:

Human Resources & Wellness:

Small Business & Financial Planning:

Adult Literacy & Learning:

Career/Retirement & Life Planning:

Distributed by:

Monogram Organizational Development Company
P.O. Box 470
Mishawaka, IN 46544-0470
(219) 255-3393